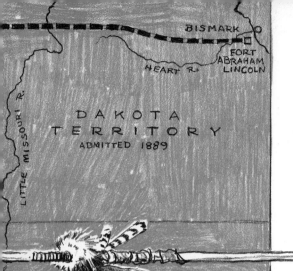

ROAD TO BATTLE

WILLIAM REUSSWIG, born in Somerville, New Jersey, got his schooling in Utica, New York and at Amherst College, where he was a member of the 1924 graduating class. Later he studied at the Art Students League, New York City. A freelance illustrator, he has worked at one time or another for most of the magazines on the market. He has traveled as Artist-War Correspondent in Europe and Asia and between assignments has visited most of the out-of-the-way corners of the world. Besides his many notable contributions in the field of pictorial art, Mr. Reusswig has published two books and several short stories. He and his wife, Martha Sawyers, live in New Milford, Connecticut.

A PICTURE REPORT OF
THE CUSTER FIGHT

by William Reusswig

HASTINGS HOUSE · PUBLISHERS

NEW YORK

*To MARTHA SAWYERS, my wife and
fellow artist and war correspondent*

CONTENTS

INTRODUCTION

SOME YEARS AGO, *Collier's* magazine commissioned artist Bill Reusswig to paint a picture of the Battle of the Little Big Horn — or, more properly, that portion of the battle that could be called the Custer Fight. Reusswig, in preparation for the assignment, spent weeks studying the battleground besides the time he devoted to the varied research necessary on uniforms, weapons, equipment and Indian regalia.

The final product of Reusswig's brush, aptly called "The Custer Fight," was published in *Collier's*, June 30, 1951. Edgar I. Stewart, noted Custer biographer (*Custer's Luck*), has pronounced it "in many respects probably the best picture of the fight . . ." The original painting — similar to the one reproduced in this book — has been displayed many times, recently in the Whitney Gallery of Western Art, Cody, Wyoming.

Ever since he did that painting, Bill Reusswig has nurtured an ambition to depict the whole battle in a series of drawings, and at long last he has done so. Readers of *A Picture Report of the Custer Fight* will be pleased and happy that the artist's long cherished plan has now become reality. That the superb drawings are complemented by a crisp descriptive commentary is additional cause for rejoicing.

DON WARD

PREFACE

THE MONTH of July 1876 was scarcely born when the nervous fingers of a white-faced dispatcher in Bismarck, Dakota Territory, tapped out a message that was to stun the people of America. "General Custer attacked the Indians June 25, and he, with every officer and man in five companies were killed. Reno with seven companies fought in intrenched position three days. The Bismark Tribune's special correspondent was with the expedition and was killed."

Seldom, if ever, has any single engagement captured the imagination of the American people as this one did. After the end of the Civil War, romance and adventure had ridden in the saddles of the "Seventh" until that shocking Sunday afternoon when the spotlight centered upon its dashing, golden-haired commander was snuffed out.

America has had its full share of colorful military leaders: men of daring and courage, marching through the pages of its history books. One of them, General George Patton, like General George Custer, was also a West Pointer with an unhappy academic record that belied his future. He commanded an Army which included a mechanized Seventh Cavalry and he too, had a consummate belief in his own destiny. Each had a flare for designing his own uniforms and carrying a favored type of fighting hardware, regardless of Army regulation. Patton wore a pair of pearl-handled revolvers; Custer packed a sporting rifle and two self-cocking English bulldog pistols. A white bull terrier was Patton's constant companion; Custer took four staghounds on his campaigns. Custer rode into battle astride "Vic," a white-stockinged, blaze-faced sorrel thoroughbred; Patton in a more businesslike tank or jeep — generally at the heads of their columns. Both men at the peak of their careers "lost face" in Army circles and were consumed with an overpowering passion to redeem hard-won fame. (Patton was almost recalled from active duty after slapping a battle-fatigued G.I. during the North African Campaign. Custer was demoted to "second-in-command" after daring to testify against President Grant's brother, who had become involved in an Army Trading Post scandal.)

These two completely fearless, kindred souls, with a disdainful contempt for any soldier who did not measure up to their own standards, were imbued with that nebulous, near-magical quality of leadership so necessary in the winning of battles. Patton survived all of his fights, but Custer's luck ran out on June 25, 1876. Two days later Lieutenant Bradley and his Indian scouts, attached to the Terry-Gibbon Command, found his naked body lying in the sun on a now famous hilltop, with the corpses of his five companies scattered, singly and in little groups, all the way down to the banks of the Little Big Horn River. No one, save the Indians, had seen them die.

So the Custer Fight will always be shrouded in mystery. The first reports of the battle were confusing and contradictory. Dozens of publicity-seekers claimed to be survivors. Reno's outfit had been too busily occupied saving its own neck to wonder about Custer's fate. The hostiles, fearing punishment by the Government, were slow to admit involvement and even when they did were apt to tell reporters what they thought the newsmen wanted to hear. Military experts combed the battlefield in an effort to reconstruct the action sequences. Pro-Custer men drew one set of conclusions from the evidence; anti-Custer men, another. Artists attempted to re-live the fight in their imagination, without the vast amounts of source material available today. Throughout the years, historians gathered thousands of items gleaned from memory books compiled by interested civilians; from letters of cavalrymen to their families, hidden away in dusty attics; from newspaper morgues; from official investigations; and from the sheer weight of oral evidence from Indians who came to the greatest massing of warriors on the American Continent, who saw the blue-coated troopers galloping to their destiny, and who conquered the flower of America's military might. Photographers, no doubt inspired by Matthew Brady of Civil War fame, went into the field, tracking down many of the participants and recording their posed portraits — for posterity.

I am grateful to all of these people, for my purpose is to produce a picture report of how the epic struggle might have *looked* at one moment during its short duration; of the characters involved; and of the events leading up to the final disaster. Even so, with the battle-dust settled for ninety-one years, the result will be a product of educated guesswork.

Chapter One
PRELUDE TO BATTLE

THE GREATEST single event leading to the battle of the Little Big Horn was the landing of the first white man upon the eastern shores of America. Indians living in the primeval wilderness bordering the coastline soon learned to resent being pushed from their campfires and shortly the early Indian wars exploded. Thousands of descendants of these woodland tribes who had padded silently through forest trails or slipped along countless waterways in their birchbark canoes ended up on the Western plains astride ponies. Here they found a new way-of-life, as well as other Indian nations already there — who also resented the white-man intrusion.

The forerunners of the white man's expansion beyond the Missouri were the breed known as "mountain men," in quest of Rocky Mountain beaver. Back east there was a great demand for beaver, for making the fashionable top-hats of the early nineteenth century. In 1803, President Thomas Jefferson sent Lewis and Clark on a trail-blazing expedition to the Pacific. A part of this famous Oregon Trail followed the North Platte and its tributary, the Sweetwater, directly through the center of the traditional buffalo-hunting ground of the great Sioux nation. When the white, canvas-topped wagons came rolling across the prairie-lands, more often than not they ran into trouble. By 1841 the pioneers were learning about safety in numbers and the first emigrant *trains* headed into the setting sun, carrying whole townsfull of assorted citizens loaded with all of their worldly goods,

unlimited expectations, and the unwitting gift of cholera and other epidemic diseases for the Indians.

Eight years later, the discovery of gold in California turned the "Great Medicine Road" into a popular highway. That same year a blond, curly-headed, ten-year-old boy named George Armstrong Custer was probably brandishing a toy pistol in a New Rumley, Ohio, backyard. His nemesis, Sitting Bull, a sturdy Indian youth of eighteen, had already proven himself a warrior and was watching with shrewd eyes the diminishing herds of buffalo that were the lifeblood of his people.

It has been estimated that the primitive count of the American buffalo ran into the fifty-millions, ranging from Buffalo, New York, to the Rocky Mountains and from Mexico well into Canada. By 1850, about twenty mil-

lion roamed the great plains west of the Mississippi and fifty years later, only a few hundred were left. For the Indians, this spelled disaster — an end to their way-of-life. The buffalo's flesh gave them strong bodies. Its horns provided them with glue, spoons, tools, and other implements, and its droppings were used as fuel. Its pelts covered their lodge poles and were turned into bed robes, leggings, moccasins, shields, bull-boats, carrying sacks and dozens of other useful objects. Bones were fashioned into fleshing tools, needles, sled runners, war clubs and axes. Even the tails were saved, for fly swatters. Its great shaggy head was used in ceremonial dances; its actions were observed and translated into portents by medicine men. And finally, its death often called for heroics that changed a boy into a man. Small wonder then that redskin warriors sat their ponies atop grassy hills, watching with fear in their hearts the plodding ox carts; the long lines of telegraph poles reaching across the prairies; the busy construction crews spiking twin rails to carry the iron monster through their heartland; and the columns of blue-coated troopers with their mule-drawn supply trains, setting up fort after fort, ever deeper into buffalo country.

As the frontier expanded westward, large tracts of land were declared open for homesteading. The dispossessed Indians were sometimes compensated by honorable agents of the government; more often they were overlooked by dishonorable agents of the same. Peace treaties were made, signed and broken. Some of the Indian chieftains recognized the inevitable

and let their people be herded onto reservations where they were allotted so many head of beef cattle to take the place of their beloved buffalo and where some of them tried to learn the art of farming. But digging roots was squaw's work, and when the spring and fall buffalo migrations showed in the dust on the far horizon, the tribe's hunters slipped away. The Indians had no way of knowing the strong, persistent pressures from gold-seekers and homesteaders that often kept the Great White Father in Washington from keeping his word. On the other side, the white man failed to realize that no one chief or group of chieftains held any real authority over any Indian nation, and had no recognized right to sign away the privileges of any individual redman. Even though in battle Indians might follow an inspired leader, they took no orders from him — and in peacetime they were sure to be at least as independent.

The western trek was slowed considerably during the Civil War, but those four bloody years quickened the yearning for glory in the breast of young Custer. It seems odd that historians so often neglect the meteoric rise of this natural-born cavalry leader who left an indelible mark at Gettysburg, the Wilderness and Shenandoah campaigns, Woodstock and Cedar Creek, Waynesboro, Five Forks and the final action at Appomattox Courthouse. The successful conclusion of his reckless, headlong cavalry charges won him major-general stars while he was scarcely more than a boy — and the envy of older officers whom he passed on his rapid climb to fame.

But peace at any time demands a price, and during the twenty-five years following the Civil War, the white and red man paid it. In 1864 Black Kettle, a chief of the Southern Cheyennes, had lost over a hundred men, women and children when Colonel Chivington's Colorado militiamen attacked his village at Sand Creek. A year later Custer, as a Lieutenant Colonel of the Seventh Cavalry, got his first taste of Indian fighting, trying to catch up with the rampaging Cheyenne, Arapaho and Kiowa warriors. He found the guerrilla tactics employed by Black Kettle and his allies completely frustrating — and took it out on his men. When some of them went AWOL and were caught, he ordered them shot without trial, and for this he was courtmartialed. Largely through the influence of General Philip Sheridan, he was re-instated.

Once back in the field, the glory-hunter surprised Black Kettle's band on the banks of the Washita, killed the chief, his wife and over a hundred warriors, burned their village and destroyed their ponies. Custer was blamed by some of his junior officers, particularly by Captain Benteen, for the loss of Major Elliot and his detachment, who were left to their fate when Custer withdrew. Custer's action may or may not have been blameworthy, but Benteen carried the bitter memory with him to the edge of disaster, eight years later. It was that same Washita fight that focused attention upon the Seventh Cavalry and returned its colorful commander to the spotlight. From that day on, his friend James Gordon Bennett, publisher of the *New York Tribune*, painted glowing word pictures of "Long Hair" and the flashing sabers of his glorious "Seventh," even suggesting that presidential timber was riding tall in the saddle.

Meanwhile, the Government decided to open up the Bozeman Trail which led northwesterly toward the headwaters of the Missouri up through the Powder River country — open it peaceably or otherwise. Now Washington was playing with fire: a fire smoldering in the eyes of a Sioux war chief named Red Cloud; and a fast-spreading prairie fire burning so deeply that ancient tribal enmities were forgotten and the Cheyennes, Arapahoes and the many clans of the mammoth Sioux nation were being fused into a common cause.

Colonel Henry B. Carrington induced Red Cloud to meet him at Fort Laramie, where he said that the Government was prepared to pay for the right to build forts along the Bozeman Trail. The chief's answer was remembered. "You are the White Eagle who has come to steal the road. The Great Father sends us presents and wants us to sell him the road, but the White Chief comes with soldiers to steal it before the Indian says yes or no. I will talk with you no more. I will go now, and I will fight you. As long as I live I will fight you for the last hunting grounds of my people."

Within six months, Colonel Carrington managed to build Fort Phil Kearny at Little Piny Fork and Fort C. F. Smith on the Big Horn River. But in all that time, he rarely had a good night's sleep. His seven hundred men of the 18th Infantry were almost continually harassed while on the march, their supply wagons raided, their beef cattle run off, mules, chickens and pigs stolen. Woodcutters outside the forts were attacked and when troops were sent to their relief they were ambushed.

On December 21, 1866, Captain Fetterman with eighty men left Fort Kearny to rescue a wood train. The young red-skinned fire-eater who decoyed them over the hill to their eternal resting place was Crazy Horse. He was one of the few Indians who was ever able to weld his individual "coup-counters" into strong striking forces operating under preconceived battle plans. Later on, nineteen soldiers fought off hundreds of Cheyennes in the "Hayfield Fight" outside Fort Smith. In another encounter, thirty-two heroes, equipped with new breechloaders and sheltered behind wagon boxes, won the day against hundreds of Sioux attackers near Fort Kearney. But the Government tried once again to settle a costly "police action" — with peace talk.

Red Cloud met the Peace Commission at Fort Laramie and touched pen with Generals Sherman, Terry and others, without ever understanding the small print. It was enough for him that the troops were withdrawn from the Bozeman Trail forts and that he was allowed to take his people back

to his Powder River homeland, setting the forts afire en route. Not long after that meeting, he was taken to Washington with some other chiefs, where he saw at first hand the power that backstopped the bluecoats. Realizing the inevitable conclusion of a continued war with the white man, he soon lost his position as a war chief. His moccasins were filled by uncompromising warriors.

On the southern plains, Colonel William Cody was hired out to supply meat for the Kansas-Pacific Railroad crews and in a seventeen-month period boasted of killing 4280 buffaloes — which failed to endear him to the native population. In the southwest, General George Crook proved his ability as an Indian fighter by digging Apaches out of their canyon hide-outs. Drovers trailed immense cattle herds up out of Texas to meet the expanding railroads for easy transportation to Eastern markets. Up north, the forts along the Yellowstone became beehives of activity as the angry Sioux buzzed around the stockades. Railroad surveyors badly needed protection, and Custer was brought north to provide it. The running fights that developed were inconclusive, and only served to stir deep-seated hatred among whites and Indians alike, as the casualties on both sides steadily mounted.

The sacred home of the Sioux deities (Pa Sapa), the Black Hills, had been closed to the whites by the 1868 Treaty, but when gold was rumored to be in the region and the reports confirmed by a Custer scouting expedition, neither soldiers nor Indians could stop the swarm of gold-seekers. The U.S. tried to buy the Black Hills from the Sioux and when this didn't work, it was decreed that all Indians not on their reservations by January 31, 1876, would be considered hostile. The Crows, who had carried on a blood feud with the Sioux, and the Arikaras joined with the whites and served as scouts with the Army. Other reservation Indians, derided as loafers by their red brothers, sought the easy way out and accepted the White Father's presents of beef and beads. But when the unscrupulous tactics of many of the Indian Agents left them half starved, thousands slipped away from the reservations to join the mounting war cry of defiance inspired by the great medicine chief, Sitting Bull.

In the southeastern United States, many families were still trying to adjust to a less aristocratic manner of life, following the Confederate defeat. In Philadelphia, a great fair was building to celebrate the first hundred years of American independence. In Chicago, General Sheridan, under orders, was devising a plan to destroy the independence of red-skinned Americans, and in Washington, the pot was beginning to boil about the Belknap scandal. Straining at the leash, Custer went to the Capitol to testify about the mistreatment of Indians and soldiers by Army Post traders. Because President Grant's brother was involved, Custer incurred the wrath of the Commander-in-Chief, was arrested for returning to his post without orders and, but for the intervention of General Sheridan, might have missed his last trek on the glory road.

Chapter Two
BATTLE PLAN

THE MAPS which General Sheridan was studying in his Chicago headquarters were not too accurate. Cartographers of the particular section of the country that interested the General had too often paid for their map-making with their scalps. His informants had told him that the mighty gathering of hostiles under Sitting Bull could be found somewhere in a triangular area twice the size of New York state, roughly bordered on the north by the Yellowstone, on the southwest by the Big Horn Mountains and on the east by the Little Missouri. Reading westward from the Little Missouri, the Powder, Tongue, Rosebud, Little Big Horn and the Big Horn rivers flowed northward into the Yellowstone. Much of the open, rolling, sage-carpeted prairie land was scarred by dry, steep-sided coulees and deep ravines. Strangely shaped, rocky escarpments between rivers and quicksands along the water courses were destined to make it rough going for an Army on the march. Here was a land jealously guarded by the Sioux — with no easy road leading to battle.

In the northwest corner, General John Gibbon commanded garrisons at Forts Benton, Cooke, Shaw and Ellis. General George Crook was stationed at Fort Fetterman, far to the south. Brigadier General Alfred Terry and Lieutenant Colonel Custer held the reins at Fort Lincoln in the east, at Bismarck, Dakota Territory.

The tri-pronged plan of attack was simple. Colonel Gibbon's Montana column would advance eastward, along the Yellowstone. General Crook's forces would march northward into the Powder River country. Custer's Dakota column would strike westward, roughly paralleling the Yellowstone. All three were scheduled to meet in the vicinity of the Big Horn River — with an unknown number of Indians caught between them. The plan would have worked, except for a few unpredictable influences like the weather, the rough nature of the country, politics, some failures to carry out orders, and the white man's underestimation of a desperate foe.

Chapter Three
JOURNEY TOWARD BATTLE

GIBBON RECEIVED his marching orders on February 27, but — because of deep snowdrifts, forty-below-zero temperatures, cases of frost-bite and snow blindness, bad communications and overturned supply wagons on the truly Rocky Mountain terrain — it was the middle of May before the various units of his command were assembled and on the trail to battle.

The Dakota Column was scheduled to leave Fort Lincoln in April but Custer was having his troubles with President Grant in Washington, and it was not until early May that Sheridan was able to get him off the hook. Consequently, Custer was second-in-command under Terry when the "Seventh" took the field on May 17 — dragging itself through a sea of mud spawned by the heavy spring rains.

Crook had already led his Indian-hunting expedition on the snowy trail north from Fort Laramie on the first day of March. A band of hostiles found his camp that night and stampeded his walking beef supply. But the "Gray Fox" established a base headquarters near the burned-out ruins of Fort Reno and continued on past Fort Kearny toward the Powder River. There he sent Colonel Reynolds forward to attack an Indian village on the banks of the river that his scouts had discovered. The camp was surprised and burned to the ground but the Cheyennes and Sioux counterattacked with such savagery that Reynolds and, in fact, Crook's whole outfit were forced to retire to Fort Fetterman. He had hit a home run a month before his team mates had taken the field, but it turned out to be a foul ball. Now the Indians were convinced that their "medicine" was good.

On May 29, just twelve days after the Dakota column had left Fort Lincoln, General Crook with a re-organized and greatly reinforced expedition, once more headed north to trade bullets with the Cheyennes and Sioux. This time he was looking for a large village said to be in the vicinity of the Rosebud. He never found it, for as it pulled up stakes and moved westward over the divide into the valley of the Little Big Horn, Crazy Horse with a force of well over a thousand Cheyenne, Blackfoot Sioux, Ogalala, Uncpapa, Sans Arc and Minneconjou Sioux warriors, rode out to meet him. And on the morning of June 17, just a hundred years after Bunker Hill, the battle of the Rosebud took place. It raged fiercely over several miles of rocky, brush-studded terrain on both sides of the river.

At day's end, the braves left Crook on the field of battle, with ten dead, twenty-one wounded, most of his ammunition expended, and short of rations. Under the circumstances, feeling that he had just encountered the full strength of the entire Sioux nation, and that the wily Crazy Horse had purposely left matters unfinished in the hope of luring him into total annihilation, the General retired southward to his base camp. A misinformed White American public rejoiced in the news of a great triumph on the Rosebud, while the Red American public on the Little Big Horn chanted victory songs. It might well have been the outcome of the Rosebud scrap that encouraged their decision to stand and fight — for by now they were aware that Gibbon, Terry and the famous "Long Hair" were looking for them.

When the "Seventh" marched out of Fort Lincoln with its band playing "The Girl I Left Behind," it was accompanied by three companies of Infantry, three Gatling guns, a large herd of cattle with drovers, a train of over 150 mule- and horse-drawn wagons, forty Arikara and Crow Indian scouts, other civilian scouts and interpreters, and four members of the Custer clan. In addition, the river steamer *Far West*, operating along the Yellowstone, carried extra supplies and would be available for ferrying troops and transporting casualties.

Twenty days and 318 miles later, Terry set up a base camp at the confluence of the Powder and Yellowstone rivers. To get there, the column had crossed swollen streams, struggled through the badlands of the Little Missouri, suffered from frost-bite one day and sunstroke the next, while mosquitoes and rattlesnakes plagued man and beast.

The "Seventh" stripped for action. Infantry remained to guard the wagon train and the mules were equipped with pack saddles. The gray horses of the band were used as mounts for one of the cavalry companies. And although the "long knives" were especially fearful to the Indians, the song of saber steel clanking against saddle leather precluded surprise attack and were therefore left behind in packing cases.

Major Reno was dispatched on a scouting mission up the Powder River, and Custer was sent cross-country to a planned rendezvous with Reno at the mouth of the Tongue.

On June 17, Reno appeared at the Rosebud, still farther west, and found Gibbon's command camping on the opposite bank of the Yellowstone. The Major had discovered a wide swath cut through the upper Rosebud country by thousands of trailing lodgepoles, evidently heading for the valley of the Little Big Horn. He knew nothing of the Crook-Crazy Horse fight which was taking place that same day. Nor did Terry, still two rivers to the east, who ordered Custer to the Rosebud and then sailed upstream on the *Far West* for a conference with Gibbon.

It was Wednesday, June 21, when Terry sent a telegram to General Sheridan in Chicago. It said: "No Indians have been met with as yet; but traces of a large and recent camp have been discovered twenty or thirty miles up the Rosebud. Gibbon's column will move this morning on the north side of the Yellowstone for the mouth of the Big Horn where it will be ferried across by the supply steamer and thence it will proceed to the mouth of the Little Horn and so on. Custer will go up the Rosebud tomorrow with his whole Regiment and thence to the headwaters and thence down the Little Horn. I hope that one of the columns will find the Indians."

Chapter Four
A LOOK AT THE "SEVENTH"

FROM ITS inception by Act of Congress, July 28, 1866, the Seventh Cavalry was destined to become one of the most distinguished regiments of the United States Army. Almost ten years later, as it took the trail up the Rosebud, it was considered the crack Indian-fighting outfit in the West. The spearpoint of fame glowed brightly about its fiery leader and filtered down through the ranks, lending an *esprit-de-corps* to even the Johnny-come-lately recruits.

The twelve troops of 585 enlisted men represented a cross-section of America at the time, including many Irish, Italian and German emigrants. There were men who had been uprooted in the East and looked westward to a new beginning. There were soldiers of fortune; ne'er-do-wells; Yankee and Rebel veterans; a few ex-convicts; some using the opportunity to get free transportation with the idea of taking "French leave" near a convenient gold field; and others trying to re-possess their shirts, lost in the Panic of 1873. These constituted the rough stock that was daily being cut and polished by a tough, hard core of "blooded" non-coms who had carved their careers with the Seventh.

Left to right, top row: Captain Tom Custer, Captain Miles Keogh, Adjutant William Cooke, Scout "Mitch" Bouyer, Interpreter Isaiah Dorman, Scout "Lonesome" Charlie Reynolds.
Second Row: "Boston" Custer, Regimental Surgeon Doctor Lord, Lieutenant James Calhoun.
Third Row: Lieutenant Charles De Rudio, Major Marcus Reno, Captain Frederick Benteen.

Except for a few eager-beavers fresh from the "Point," most of the officers were veterans of combat, either in the Civil War or in Indian fights, or both. Some, like their leader, had received their formal military training at the Academy; others had worked up from the ranks and had won recognition in the field. One of the latter, Custer's younger brother, Captain Tom, cherished two Congressional Medals of Honor. Major Marcus Reno and Captain Fred Benteen, because of real or fancied ill treatment by their Commander, led an anti-Custer faction. Both, however, were proven warriors although the former had never tasted the bitter cup of frustration served up by the hit-and-run Indian tactics. Included among the officers were half-breed Mohawk Indian Lieutenant McIntosh; Lieutenant Sturgis, son of the "Seventh's" inactive Commander; Lieutenant Cooke, a Canadian soldier-of-fortune; Lieutenant De Rudio, who had fought with Garibaldi for Italian independence; Captains Keogh and Nolan, formerly of the Papal Guard, and Calhoun, married to Mrs. Custer's sister; and Doctors Lord, De Wolf and Porter. Signed on as "forage-master," the Colonel's youngest brother "Boston" Custer, had, ironically, come along for his health; and a nephew Autie Reed, nicknamed after his famous uncle and listed as "herder," was taking a summer outing. Unwittingly Mark Kellogg, special correspondent, was sticking his nose for news into real trouble.

With the Seventh rode a detachment of forty Arikara and six Crow scouts. Their job was to lead the way, fanning out ahead of the Column to forestall possible ambush and finally, when brought to engagement with the foe, to run off the enemy pony herds. Girard, the interpreter, acted as go-between. Also with the scouting detail were "Mitch" Bouyer, "Lonesome" Charlie Reynolds, Billy Jackson, George Herendeen and a Negro scout, Isaiah Dorman. All of them had Sioux "savvy," knew the country, and had a high respect for the fighting qualities of the enemy.

The pack train of 175 mules carried fifteen days' rations of hard bread, salt, sugar, coffee, bacon, and fifty rounds of carbine ammunition for each trooper. On his person, or strapped to his McClellan saddle, the cavalryman toted 100 rounds of ammunition for his single-shot carbine, twenty-four rounds of pistol ammunition and twelve pounds of oats.

At a last-minute conference with Terry and Gibbon, the latter told Custer: "Don't be greedy — leave a few Indians for the rest of us." Apparently they had agreed that the reports of their scouts were greatly exaggerated — and that the warrior strength of the enemy numbered not more than 1500, which they were confident either column could handle, even if they failed to meet at the appointed tryst on the Little Big Horn. Their only worry was that the foe would flee for the Big Horn Mountains to the south and scatter into small bands before they could ever catch up with them. They failed to appreciate one single fact that outweighed all others — that the Sioux and Cheyennes, driven by desperation, had sworn to run no more, but would fight like cornered grizzlies for their beloved hunting grounds. Had not the Everywhere Spirit given the great Sitting Bull a vision of many mounted bluecoats tumbling upside down into their camp?

Chapter Five
A LOOK AT THE LITTLE BIG HORN INDIAN CAMP

THE CHETISH or Wolf Mountains separate the valleys of the Rosebud and the Little Big Horn. Hardly rating as mountains, they are hilly outcroppings, sculptured into fantastic shapes by the erosive action of wind and water. One of the loftier promontories in the divide is called the "Crow's Nest," and there is nothing nautical in the name. From this spot, the Crow Indians could keep tabs on the migrating buffalo herds, as well as a watchful outlook for Sioux interlopers.

West of the divide, the Little Big Horn snakes its serpentine course across a wide valley, in a northerly direction to its junction with the Big

Horn. Some of its coils swing toward the rising series of benchlands in the west; others snuggle against steep, eastern bluffs that are so abrupt as to be impassable except where infrequent creek beds have been blasted through to the mother stream. The river itself, from two to five feet deep, runs clear and cold over a pebbly bottom between soft but perpendicular banks, twenty to forty yards apart. Groves of cottonwood and box elder mark its course across an otherwise treeless, wide open plain.

Across the river from the bluffs, the lodges of the hostiles were pitched in seven great camp circles, each about half a mile in diameter; collectively covering a broad area over four miles long. A census of this nomad city might well have given the impatient Custer pause for sober thought.

49 · A LOOK AT THE LITTLE BIG HORN INDIAN CAMP

INDIANS	CHIEFTAINS
Cheyennes (north end of camp)	Two Moon, Little Horse, Dirty Mocassins, Old Bear, Crazy Head, Lame White Man, Old Man Coyote, Last Bull, Little Wolf
Ogalala Sioux	Big Road, He Dog, Crazy Horse
Brulé Sioux	Crow Dog
Sans-arc Sioux	Spotted Eagle, Fast Bear
Two Kettle Sioux	Runs the Enemy
Minneconjou Sioux	Lame Deer, Hump, Fast Bull, High Backbone
Santee Sioux	Inkpaduta
Blackfoot Sioux	Scabby Head
Hunkpapa Sioux (farthest south)	Gall, Crow King, Black Moon, Sitting Bull, Rain-in-the-Face

Early, wild guesses of the population of this, the greatest massing of Indians ever on the American Continent, ran well into five figures, including 10,000 warriors. Later, careful estimates by students of the Custer Battle brought the fighting strength down to about 4000 — which still outnumbered Custer's force by eight to one. Some fortunate few carried repeating, lever-action rifles, captured or bartered from the white man. Many others were armed with ancient muzzle-loaders, pistols, spears, war clubs, bows and arrows. The latter, in the hands of these experts, could be much more effective repeaters than the standard single-shot, cavalry carbines. But their most potent weapon was supreme confidence in their "medicine."

51 · A LOOK AT THE LITTLE BIG HORN INDIAN CAMP

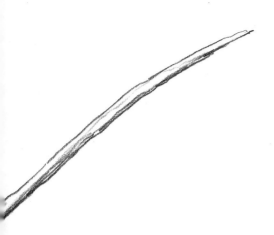

Chapter Six
THE TRAIL WARMS UP

IF CUSTER had any disturbing second thoughts concerning what lay ahead, there was no indication of it as he waved a jaunty farewell, touched spurs to Vic, and cantered off to overtake his command.

At eight o'clock in the evening of Saturday, the 24th, the Regiment camped at the junction of Thompson's Creek with the Rosebud, approximately seventy-five miles upstream from the Yellowstone. Pack mules, horses, and the men, save one, were wearied to the edge of exhaustion. The weather had turned very hot — but so had the great Indian trail they had located on the previous day. Here the whole valley bottom was churned up from thousands of travois, and a series of large campsites were strewn with bones and bits of fresh buffalo hide, broken and discarded implements, pony droppings and, at one, the framework of a sun-dance lodge with the scalp of a white man hanging from the peak. Sand pictures of dead soldiers with their heads pointing toward a Sioux camp, clearly indicated that the hostiles were aware of a coming battle — and predicted its outcome. Curious arrangements of stones and buffalo skulls gave a like message to Custer's Crow and Arikara scouts.

But far from inspiring caution, these signs of warning only served as fuel to the restless energy of the Seventh's commander. In spite of the fact that at this point he was twenty-four hours ahead of schedule and that his outfit was in dire need of rest, he dispatched three Indian scouts to the Crow's Nest and warned his staff of a probable night march. Within the hour, the scouts reported that they had not been able to see any signs of the enemy camp, but that the trail definitely led up over the divide into the valley of the Little Big Horn. Custer then advised his officers that they would march at 11 o'clock that night and camp near the top of the divide. His plan was to spend all of Sunday reconnoitering the valley, and to attack at daybreak on Monday, providing the Sioux were within reach. In the meantime, he sent Lieutenant Varnum, Bouyer, Reynolds and ten Indian scouts back to the Crow's Nest.

At the end of the conference, some of the younger officers, having been told they were in for the fight of their lives, celebrated the occasion by harmonizing "Annie Laurie" and, stretching a point, "For He's a Jolly Good Fellow." They couldn't have known that two Cheyenne warriors of Little Wolf's band were listening in from deep cover, close by. For the hidden audience, this was obviously some sort of white man's medicine.

Because of delay caused by the mules that were trained to the traces rather than as pack animals, it was the first hour of that fateful Sunday by the time the Regiment started to move up the divide. The narrow, rocky defile to the headwaters of Davis Creek allowed only single-file passageway and the troopers on the dust-clogged, moonless trail pounded on their tin cups to signal their course. Several hours and only six miles later, the entire command was hidden away in a heavily wooded, high-walled canyon.

Excitement mounted at the Crow's Nest as the clear, cold light of daybreak revealed hundreds of tiny, white, triangular specks along the winding Little Big Horn, fifteen miles across the prairie. The smoke of lodge fires hung heavy over the river and billowing dust clouds above the western bench lands marked the grazing ground of an enormous pony herd. But by the time Custer arrived at the lookout, the sun had climbed well into the heavens and shimmering heat waves bouncing off the valley floor obscured the view. Even with the aid of Bouyer's fieldglasses, the Commander was stubbornly unconvinced. Events were shortly to change his attitude. The Crow scouts reported that they had seen six mounted Sioux riding from the base of the hills toward their camp, pausing to circle their ponies, which signaled to their friends the nearness of soldiers. They had evidently spotted the smoke rising from the Seventh's camp, which was clearly visible from the Crow's Nest.

Returning to his command, Custer learned that three troopers searching the back trail for some bread boxes lost from the pack train had found an Indian trying to open one of them. He had flung himself onto his pony and galloped out of range. A messenger from the Crow's Nest brought news of still another Indian camp on the march downstream, apparently alerted by the circling Sioux scouts. So the timetable was advanced again. Since the element of surprise was lost and the enemy *seemed* to be running away, Custer decided to attack at once.

Seven men from each company were delegated to help guard the pack train, which was to follow after a twenty-minute interval. Indian scouts were sent ahead to steal or scatter the enemy horse herd. White-Man-Runs-Him loped his pony up the last slope of the lodgepole trail. Behind him, Mark Kellogg rode his runty, gray mule alongside Custer's prancing mare. And with a devil-may-care flourish of trumpets, the Seventh swung into line. At high noon, the column crossed over the crest of the divide and headed down into the valley of the Little Big Horn.

A mile farther on, near the headwaters of Reno Creek, Custer called a halt in order to dispatch Captain Benteen with three companies off to the left to scout a line of bluffs and to pitch into any Indians he could find. The Colonel evidently hoped by this maneuver to block an enemy dash for the safety of the Big Horn Mountains. It was here too, that scout "Mitch" Bouyer told him, "If we go in there we will never come out," and received an explosive blast of the famous Custer temper for his pains.

On the move again, Major Reno with three companies was ordered to proceed in columns of fours along the left bank while Custer, leading the remaining five troops, kept pace with him on the right bank.

We know now that it was about two o'clock when they reached the handsomely decorated "Lone Warrior Tepee," containing the body of a Sans-arc warrior known as "Old She Bear." Dressed in his beaded and feathered finery, with his face painted red after death, this casualty from Crook's Rosebud battle was the only Sioux in sight. The Crow and Arikara scouts who had understandably hesitated to stir up the hornet's nest that lay ahead were ordered once more to get on with their appointed task. Hidden from view behind an intercepting cottonwood grove, and projecting river bluffs, the exact size and location of the monster nomad city was still unknown to Custer. But his scouts were well aware that "There were more Sioux ahead than there were bullets in the belts of the soldiers."

Custer ordered Reno to proceed downstream, ford the Little Big Horn at the nearest point and immediately attack the Indian encampment. Custer would, he added, support Reno with the whole outfit. His probable intention at that moment was to follow up his major's initial strike from the rear. But soon after he sent Reno into battle, Lieutenant Varnum returned from a scout along the eastern bluffs with an eye-witness account of at least a part of the hostile camp a few miles downstream. Varnum hurried off to rejoin the main body of scouts who had gone ahead of Reno, and Custer took the high trail, evidently hoping to cross a ford at the north end of the village and to roll up the Sioux between the two commands.

Chapter Seven
RENO DRAWS FIRST BLOOD

AT 2:30 in the afternoon Reno's three companies forded the Little Big Horn. While their mounts lingered to drink the cool, crystalline river water and the soldiers leaned from their saddles to refill their canteens, scout Girard galloped up to the Major and advised him that many Indians were riding upstream to meet him. Trooper McIllhargy was dispatched to Custer with the message: "Enemy in front and very strong." Then the men were reformed in the narrow belt of timber beside the ford, and trotted out in columns of four abreast with the heads of the three companies on a line. After half a mile, the formation was changed, with A and M forming a line abreast with G in reserve. And finally, as the threatening dust storm up ahead exploded with racing wraiths, Reno brought up G and led his cheering bluecoats at a headlong gallop into combat.

65 • RENO DRAWS FIRST BLOOD

Had the situation been reversed, and the Sioux had been attacking a pre-warned camp of white soldiers, there would have been an organized plan of battle, ready to receive the visitors. As it was, the Hunkpapa circle at the southernmost end of the village was a scene of wild confusion as Reno's charge was seen rolling down the valley. After all, *dawn* was the accepted time for attack — not in the heat of early afternoon. Many warriors who were still out hunting swung their ponies about in a mad dash for home, when the first scattered shots signaled the beginning of the battle. Old folks and cripples left their meager belongings behind and hobbled northward as fast as their weary legs could carry them. Some of the women who had been digging tipsin (wild turnips) at the river edge ran about screaming to gather their children.

CROW KING

LOW DOG

GALL

Earlier in the day Sitting Bull had been in council, trying diplomatically to settle a dispute between his own people and a band of Blackfoot Sioux who had declared their intention of returning to the Agency. Two outstanding white-man haters, Rain-in-the-Face and Crow King, had been present. These chieftains, as well as all of the other great leaders in the tepee city knew that "Longhair" was in the vicinity. They also knew his strength to a man, and that the Terry-Gibbon command was a two-day journey away, to the northwest. Most of all, they knew their own fighting power and were confident — as well they might have been.

But with the first hint of danger, the war cry "Hoka-hey" rang through the camp. Sitting Bull mounted a favorite black stallion and galloped among the tents to "brave-up" his warriors. He sent his nephew, One Bull, to try to parley with the soldiers or, failing that, to fight a delaying action. Gall quickly gathered a band of Hunkpapas: "Take courage. Don't be women. The helpless are out of breath." It was probably his organized attack that sent the first chill of uncertainty fluttering through Reno's chest. Some, like Iron Hawk, lingered long enough to braid eagle feathers into their hair. At the Ogalala camp, Crazy Horse casually painted his naked torso with yellow-ochre hail spots before summoning his clan with a "Hiyupo." Black Moon marshaled his Fox Warriors who were on camp police duty, and led them westward where Reno's Arikara scouts had managed to cut out some of the Sioux pony herd.

CRAZY HORSE

SITTING BULL

This was the Major's first encounter on his own with the frustrating fury of Indian fighting. Out of the choking dust clouds up ahead, bands of feathered fiends appeared like magic, traded bullets with his men, wheeled their ponies, and evaporated into the ghostly swirl of battle. If Reno had carried out his orders, he *might* have allowed Custer a chance to wreck the power of the Sioux for all time. He also might have added his own body and those of his 134 officers and men to the impending carnage on Custer Hill. He didn't. Instead, within a hundred yards of the smoke-blackened tips of the Hunkpapa tepees and seeing no sign of Custer in his rear, he called a halt, dismounted his troopers and formed them into a line of skirmishers on foot. Every fourth man remained mounted and led the horses of three of his companions to the cover of a cottonwood grove which extended out from the river bank to within fifty yards of the right flank. It was during this maneuver that four of the untrained animals bolted into the Indian lines and were immediately swallowed up. By a strange fluke of fate

which so often occurs in battle, two of them returned still carrying their riders, wounded but alive. The abrupt end of the charge not only cut down Reno's firepower, but negated the use of his cavalry as a mobile, offensive weapon; placed him in a vulnerable, defensive position: and encouraged the Sioux to redouble their efforts. For the Indians, "This was a good day to die."

Spaced at five-yard intervals, the thin line of less than a hundred skirmishers deployed for a quarter of a mile out toward the benchlands. For a few more desperate moments, they advanced slowly, maintaining such a rapid rate of fire that carbines overheated and it became difficult to extract spent cartridges. Some of their bullets penetrated Gall's tent, killing two wives and three children. But with every man firing at will, it soon became necessary to send alternate troopers back to retrieve ammunition from the saddlebags. Then as the Sioux started to infiltrate the cottonwood grove to get at the cavalry horses, the remainder of G Company was withdrawn to protect them. Meanwhile, out toward the benchlands, Black Moon's Fox Warriors had recaptured most of their stolen ponies, killing three of Reno's Arikara scouts and scattering the rest. And when they outflanked the left of the skirmishers' line, the Major ordered the rest of his command to retreat to the timber.

About twenty minutes had elapsed since Reno had halted his charge. Now, at approximately three o'clock, Lieutenants Varnum and De Rudio caught a glimpse of Custer on the high bluffs across the river. Sitting Bull, suspecting a trap when Reno failed to follow through, also saw Custer, knew exactly how long it would take him to reach Minneconjou Ford at the base of Medicine Tail Coulee, and set his own trap for the bluecoats. Captain Benteen, having found no Indians in the western hills, was swinging back to rejoin Custer. Captain McDougall's pack train was moving slowly down the western slope of the divide, following the lodgepole trail. Far to the northwest, troops of the Terry-Gibbon command were helping to "warp" the *Far West* up through the swollen rapids of the Big Horn, while scouts were searching out a short cut to the Little Big Horn, via Tulloch's Creek. General Crook, the most experienced Indian fighter of them all, was nursing his wounds many miles to the south, completely out of the picture.

At first, the shelter of the timber was a welcome relief from the open prairie. A cut bank, left by one of the frequent changes of course of the Little Big Horn, afforded good protection along a part of its perimeter, where the troopers could dig in. Behind it, elder thickets and heavier cottonwoods concealed the men from the circling warriors, who were constantly growing in numbers and displaying a recklessness born of a belief in their day of destiny. While the feathered horsemen kept Reno's troopers busy on the open prairie sides of the timber, dismounted Sioux forded the river and crept within a few yards of their hated foe before announcing their presence with volleys of bullets and arrows.

Reno was hatless now, with a handkerchief tied around his head to keep hair and sweat from his eyes. In a small clearing in the center of the woods, he sat his charger, trying desperately to plan his next move. Neither

Varnum nor De Rudio had had the opportunity of informing their commander that they had seen some of Custer's gray-horse troop on the bluff overlooking the river. The Major listened for a distant trumpet call that never sounded. After half an hour of mounting tension, he decided that the best chance of saving his battalion lay in reaching the high ground across the Little Big Horn. He would lead his men upstream to his original fording place and then back along the bluffs. Up there, perhaps, Custer would be able to see him, from wherever he was.

Reno shouted the order for his command to regroup in the clearing. Some of the troops were too busily occupied to obey the order, even if they could have heard it above the battle din. While the others were gathering, firing by the soldiers abated, and a large party of Sioux broke into the clearing within ten yards of the command. One of the troopers wilted in his saddle. Indian scout Bloody Knife was struck between the eyes, splattering blood over Reno's face. In the wild melee of the next few moments pistol

butts and stone axes were brought into play and the wonder of it was that so many troopers survived to follow their leader crashing through the thickets, once more onto the open prairie. Here the swarming hordes, refusing to meet a head-on charge, swung aside and raced along the right flank, crowding the battalion ever closer to the river bank. Some of the Sioux clung to the off sides of their mustangs, shooting from underneath their ponies' heads. Others simply placed their rifles at right angles across the withers and pumped lead into the troops. Still others, watching for the moment when a trooper needed to reload, attempted to club or wrestle the enemy off his horse.

The high-pitched, staccato war cries; the screams of wounded men and horses; the shrill notes of eagle-bone whistles used by the Sioux in battle; the close-ranged gunfire and the quick song of bullets ending in meaty slaps as they found targets were the answers to a call to charge that turned into a stampede. For the Indians, "It was as easy as running buffalo."

Some of the buffaloes fought back. Captain Moylan, along with Lieutenants Varnum and De Rudio, at least attempted to organize rear-guard actions to prevent the hostiles from completely overrunning the soldiers in their headlong flight upriver. The famous scout, Charlie Reynolds, was cut off from the fleeing command. His horse was shot out from under him and he met a lonesome death, the ground about him littered with spent cartridges. There is no record of the number of Sioux who took the final trek with him to a new hunting ground. Isaiah Dorman, Negro interpreter who had lived among the Sioux for many years, went down en route to the river. His bullet-riddled mount, threshing about in its death struggle, rolled on top of him, leaving his wounded and broken body a prey for the vengeful Sioux women. Lieutenant McIntosh, the part-blood Mohawk, rounded up sixteen troopers left behind in the timber and tried to rejoin the command. All kept a date with destiny, but not with Reno. Varnum's orderly was wounded and unhorsed. The Lieutenant reined in and with the aid of two soldiers caught a loose animal and remounted his man. Lieutenant Wallace tried to save a

downed trooper in a like manner, but the man was killed before he was able to climb into the saddle. In the course of one soul-chilling mile, many men, pushed beyond the barrier of fear, performed acts of heroism that later became legends among their bunk mates. And that same mile produced a whole new crop of coup-counters in the ranks of the redmen.

Overwhelming pressure against the right flank turned the van of the column onto the bank of the Little Big Horn, several miles short of Reno's original crossing. Here was a take-it-or-leave-it ford. The frantic horses, most of them out of control, simply leaped or were pushed from behind off the six-foot crumbling cliff into saddle-deep water. Many Sioux rabbit-jumped their nimble ponies alongside, carrying the hand-to-hand fight right into the river. Its usual, cool, green-blue surface, a reflection of the summer sky and the full foliage of the cottonwoods, carried a new, pinkish tinge downstream.

Lieutenant Benny Hodgson, who was Reno's adjutant and one of the most popular officers in the entire Seventh, was shot through the leg and catapulted from the saddle as his mount took flight from the west bank. His life was spared for a moment by a trooper who offered his stirrup strap, towing him across the river. It was lost as Hodgson, too weak to climb out of the water, turned to empty his revolver for the last time.

The cavalry horses swam or waded wherever they could catch a slippery footing, carrying their harried riders over the longest stretch of fifty feet of open water in the world. Exposed to a deadly sniper fire from the bluffs ahead of them and faced with a perpendicular eight-foot east bank, the odds for survival must have seemed insurmountable to most of the men. And yet, somehow, they scrambled out of the river and followed their leader up through a steep ravine to gain the heights a hundred feet above the bottom land.

Acting Surgeon De Wolf climbed the wrong ravine and paid for his error with his scalp. The doctor wasn't alone, for the race course all the way back to the edge of the Hunkpapa village was clearly marked by the bodies of Seventh Cavalry men and horses. Reno had lost over a third of his command in dead, wounded and missing. The time was now almost four o'clock, and as the last weary stragglers looked back from their vantage point over the combat road they might have enjoyed a momentary sense of relief at seeing hundreds of Sioux horsemen riding downstream — away from the battle.

Chapter Eight
GOOSE CHASE

CAPTAIN FRED BENTEEN, with his three companies totaling about 125 men, had despaired of catching any wild geese in the western benchlands, and was swinging back to rejoin the regiment. Just before they reached the Lodgepole trail, Boston Custer galloped by on a fresh mount obtained from the pack train a mile in the rear. He was in a hurry to catch up with his brother; worried, like any true member of the Custer clan, that he might miss some of the excitement that lay ahead.

As his detachment trotted past the Lone Warrior's tepee which was still burning from a vengeful torch applied by one of Custer's scouts or troopers, Benteen was unaware of the fact that Custer had split his command a second time and that Reno was already up to his neck in hostiles. A mile beyond the tepee Sergeant Kanipe arrived with an oral message from Captain Tom Custer for Captain McDougal — to hurry cross-country with the pack train. Since that was no concern of Benteen's, the sergeant was sent on his way to the rear. The next encounter was with Trumpeter Martin, who reined up beside Benteen on a spent and badly wounded horse and handed him a hastily scrawled note from Custer's Adjutant Cooke: *Benteen — come on — big village — be quick — bring packs.* W. W. COOKE. *P.S. Bring packs.*

Trumpeter Martin added a personal touch, telling Benteen that the Indians had "skedaddled" and that he thought by now that Custer was probably charging through the big camp.

On the move again, the troopers soon heard gunfire echoing through the valley up ahead. But due to interceding bluffs and rocky foothills, they hadn't been able to see what was going on. Now suddenly, they caught a distant view of the southern end of the Indian village. It appeared that two fights were raging at the same time, one along the valley floor and another on the bluffs above it. Benteen could see figures of friend and foe alike, racing upstream under a heavy pall of battle smoke. It seemed to him that if anyone was "skedaddling" it was a thin line of blue heading for the bluffs. This first indication that all was not well was confirmed by a handful of Arikara pony rustlers who rode up shouting; "Otoe Sioux, Otoe Sioux — big pooh-poohing" (Heaps of Sioux and big fight going on.)

Benteen decided that the quickest way to rejoin the regiment was to take the high trail leading up behind the bluffs, instead of following the Reno trail into the valley. He put away his pipe, quickened his pace and reached Reno Hill just as the last of the Major's men were straggling up the ravine. Reno rode out to meet him.

"For God's sake, Benteen, halt your command and help me. I've lost half my men."

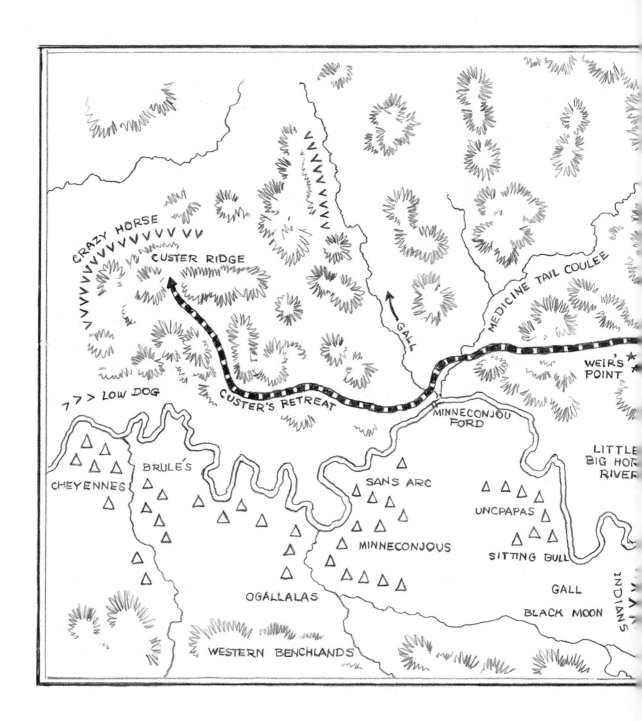

CRAZY HORSE

CUSTER RIDGE

MEDICINE TAIL COULEE

GALL

WEIR'S POINT

CUSTER'S RETREAT

7 7 > LOW DOG

MINNECONJOU FORD

LITTLE BIG HORN RIVER

CHEYENNES

BRULE'S

SANS ARC

UNCPAPAS

INDIANS

MINNECONJOUS

SITTING BULL

OGALLALAS

GALL

BLACK MOON

WESTERN BENCHLANDS

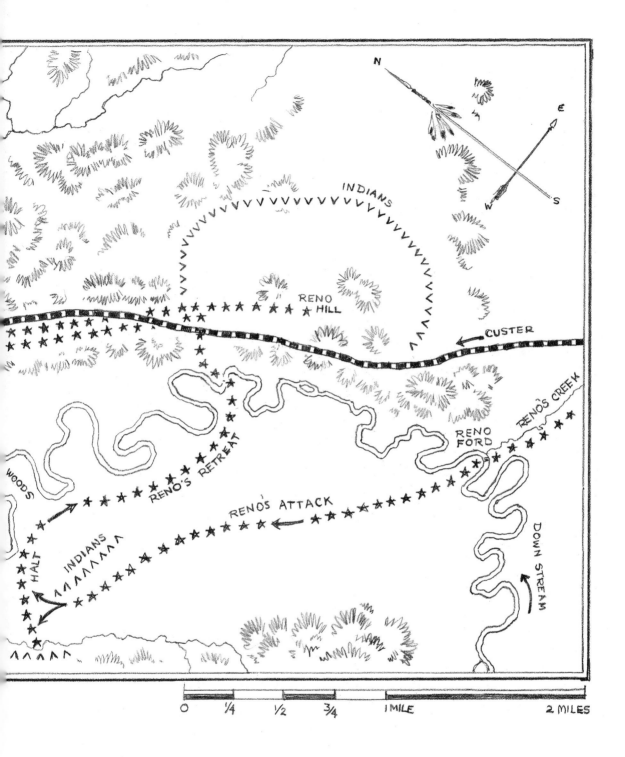

N

E

W

S

INDIANS

RENO
HILL

CUSTER

RENO'S CREEK

RENO
FORD

WOODS

RENO'S RETREAT

RENO'S ATTACK

DOWN STREAM

HALT

INDIANS

O   ¼   ½   ¾   1 MILE   2 MILES

93 • GOOSE CHASE

Chapter Nine
APPROACH TO DISASTER

AT THE time America's Public Hero No. 1 ordered Reno to attack the Indian village, he probably intended to support his Major from the rear. The open plains west of the river afforded the best chance to maneuver his cavalry, while the rough country above and beyond the bluffs was suspect for possible ambush. Varnum, scouting ahead of the command, had reported seeing many Indians and a large camp in the bottom land. If he had gone far enough to get an accurate picture of the extent and fighting strength of the great nomad city, he probably would never have returned. Bouyer and the Crow scouts who had lived and hunted in this area knew of the shallow dip following behind the crest of the bluffs which led after three or four miles to Medicine Tail Coulee. The coulee cut sharply down through the rocky ramparts to its juncture with the river at Minneconjou Ford.

It was probably this knowledge which caused Custer to change his plans. He would follow this route, cross at the north end of the village, and box the enemy between his own and Reno's forces. By now, he was no doubt aware of the fact that he was in for the fight of his life. But he was obsessed with the idea that the Sioux and Cheyennes might get away from him and scatter into small bands among the Big Horn Mountains to the southwest. He was willing to lay his famous Custer luck on the line once more.

At the head of his five companies, F, C, E, I and L, Custer swung right off the main Lodgepole trail and paused at the north branch of Reno's creek to water his horses. Trooper McIlhargy found him there and reported from Reno that he had crossed the Little Big Horn and that the Sioux were

swarming upstream to meet him. To the Colonel this could mean only one thing; the Indians were breaking camp and running for the hills, sending back warriors to protect the retreat of their women and children. Impatient for a head-on collision with the enemy, he led his troops up over a ridge at a fast clip and turned downstream behind the bluffs. He galloped past the hill where Reno would dig in within the hour.

Twice along the route to Medicine Tail Coulee, he halted his men for quick, personal side excursions to the top of the bluffs. On the first trip he saw several hundred lodges, which in truth only represented a small part of the encampment. From this high point (near the Hodson marker) he was in a position to observe Reno's charge down the valley. Here was a good-sized battle in the making; one which might well call for extra ammunition. So, through his brother Tom Custer, he gave an oral message to Sergeant Kanipe and sent him on the back trail to bring up McDougal's pack train. For a mile

after this first pause, the parade proceeded at such a fast clip that four horses dropped from exhaustion. Two of their riders subsequently managed to reach Reno Hill. The others were declared missing in action.

It was after three o'clock when Custer rode out onto the cliff edge the second time, in the vicinity of Weir's Point. With him were Captain Tom, Adjutant Cooke, Autie Reed and Trumpeter Martin. The village below them seemed deserted except for women, children, dogs and a few ponies. Reno's command was out of sight (probably in the timber), a fact which didn't seem to disturb the Colonel. In the distance, upstream, a dust cloud indicated that Benteen was coming up on the back trail; and another, that the pack train was a mile or so behind him. He dispatched Trumpeter Martin to "hurry up" Benteen and the packs and, with a flourish of his big, white hat, galloped off to set his command in motion. His hat-waving gesture was observed by both friendly and hostile eyes, deep in the valley.

Since Trumpeter Martin was a young Italian boy with a limited vocabulary, Adjutant Cooke hastily scribbled the order on a slip of paper. As the courier rode off he turned in his saddle and saw Custer's command heading toward Medicine Tail Coulee. Almost at once he encountered Boston Custer, who inquired the whereabouts of his brother and then raced off to join his fate. And as Martin galloped about his business, he heard the opening chorus of gunfire and saw a handful of Sioux warriors, flushed from cover by the Crow scouts, fire a few rounds at the soldiers and wave buffalo robes to stampede the cavalry horses. His later, garbled account carried some conviction because an enemy bullet found his sturdy mount, which was still able to carry him over the back trail, past Reno's mad scramble below the bluffs, all the way down to Benteen's command. He was the last white survivor to see Custer alive.

Chapter Ten
REDMAN'S RECEPTION COMMITTEE

THE INDIANS had no blueprint for battle such as the white man employed under similar circumstances. There was no supreme general among all the renowned chiefs present who had the authority to assume overall command and to co-ordinate a combined firepower when and where it would be most effective. But they had known for days the movements of the bluecoats and there can be no doubt that men like Sitting Bull, Gall, Crazy Horse, Crow King, and a score of others had discussed some loose plan for receiving their visitors.

Their strategy hung upon two circumstances. First, they had long ago decided to stand and fight — and therefore must keep the impending battle *out* of their village. Second, the high ground across the river, being a series of sage- and brush-covered hills bisected by innumerable dry coulees and steep ravines, afforded natural cover for hundreds or even thousands of warriors, both mounted and on foot. In particular, there were two ravines originating close together several hundred yards north and east of the Little Big Horn. The eastern one wound down to its junction with the river near Medicine Tail Coulee; the other, swinging in a wide western arc, debouched into the river at a spot known as the Cheyenne Ford, beyond the northernmost camp circle. Between the two, a long hogback rises from the bottom land to a ridge where a stone slab today marks the spot of "The Last Stand."

The only element of surprise lay in the timing of Reno's attack. The Indians had seen the "Seventh" marching down the western slope of the divide, knew of the double split in the command and, as Custer hurried along the high road, many hundreds of pairs of hostile eyes were watching him from closer concealment than he ever could have suspected. A large band of Sioux lurked in the heavily thicketed timber growth facing Medicine Tail Coulee. Gall had raced upstream to spearpoint the attack against Reno, had stopped him cold in his tracks, and driven him up onto Reno Hill. Now he crossed over, climbed the bluffs, left enough force to contain Reno, and swung about in the wake of Custer's column. Crow King spirited a company of several hundred warriors up the eastern ravine that skirted Custer Ridge.

Crazy Horse, having started to attack Reno, saw Custer on the bluffs, doubled back and headed downstream, gathering the main body of Ogalalas and Cheyennes en route. He crossed at Cheyenne Ford and sped up the western coulee that bounded the far side of Custer Ridge. Another band, led by Iron Star and Low Dog, followed Crazy Horse across the river and immediately cut back, getting into position between the ridge and the river. And as if this was not enough, there were late arrivals and unattached "loners," including at least one woman, who climbed up on foot or horseback through numerous other coulees — to be in on the kill.

If the nature of the country had permitted Custer to see the monster mass of warriors which completely surrounded his command, arrayed in their finery as a token of their readiness to meet death, a premonition of disaster might have tempered some of his eager spirit.

OVERLEAF: "The Custer Fight," painting by William Reusswig

Chapter Eleven
THE FINISH FIGHT

As THE column trotted down the slippery shale footing of Medicine Tail
Coulee, Mitch Bouyer told the youngest Crow scout Curley to stay out of
the fight, to watch it for a while from the bluffs and then to search out "No
Hips" Terry. And shortly, the three remaining Crow scouts, Hairy Moccasin,
Goes Ahead and White-Man-Runs-Him, were ordered by Custer to go back
to the pack train. What they witnessed from the high ground overlooking
Minneconjou Ford has long been a subject of controversy, but there can be
little doubt that they saw the beginning of the end of Custer's last stand. If
they had lingered for a time lapse of fifteen to forty-five minutes, they might
have seen the final curtain drop over the nearby dust- and smoke-shrouded
hill top.

The buffalo-robe-waving decoys turned off a side canyon away from the Indian camp. Custer, familiar with this old trick, grimly led his five troops down to the mouth of the coulee, where he momentarily halted the command as it received a blistering fire from an unseen foe hidden in the heavy cover on the opposite bank. With his troops in column stretching back up the canyon, he was unable to return an effective counterfire, so he swung right, hoping to ford the river downstream in more open country. Companies F, C and E, under Yates, Tom Custer and Smith, followed him in staggered echelon along the western slope of the hogback. Here, under mounting pressure from Iron Star and Low Dog, he was forced away from the stream toward the crest of the ridge. On his right, being farthest away from Minneconjou Ford when the order to turn right was relayed back to them, Keogh's I Company and Calhoun's L Company also climbed in the direction of Custer Ridge, where they met the full impact of Gall's attack, roaring up from the back trail. Calhoun's company was ordered to dismount and to deploy as skirmishers, so that the rest of the command could reach the high ground. And not far beyond him, Keogh followed suit, to cover Calhoun.

Calhoun supplied only temporary relief for the remainder of the battalion. The survivors of his company who had lived to deploy along that hillside fought with the fierce abandon of despair, firing overheated carbines and then swinging them as clubs when defective cartridges jammed the breeches. Gall's whirlwind charge smashed them into the earth where, today, a straggling line of markers tells their heroic story.

The chief's triumphant war cry echoed above the din of battle as he regrouped and swung around to lead the assault against Keogh. The Captain went down with a bullet-shattered leg and his company sergeants gathered about their leader in a futile effort to save his life. Then as the dozen or so remaining troopers were ordered to rejoin Custer, they were toppled into oblivion and Company I's guidon fluttered down the slope in the hands of a mounted warrior.

By now the White Chief was in the most serious predicament of his career. Under constant fire since leaving the ford, he should have known that each passing second pronounced his doom. Lieutenant Smith's Company E had been deployed halfway up the hogback's western slope and had been cut to pieces almost before they had dismounted. And as the depleted ranks of C and F neared the crest of Custer Ridge, they found hundreds of Ogalalas and Cheyennes under the wily Crazy Horse waiting for them. Surrounded from the very beginning of the finish fight, forty blue-shirted troopers and a handful of buckskin-clad officers felt the red noose tightening about their throats. In every direction, yelping, victory-eager warriors swirled through the heavy smoke-screen, darting in and out again on foot and on horseback, hardly bothering to aim their weapons.

For a brief while longer (who knows its duration?) the diminishing band, clustered about Custer's personal battle pennant within a ring of dead horses, made their stand. Then as they wilted into the dust, a final Indian rush crushed what life was left. Scattered shots continued for half an hour as the victors rode over the battlefield, firing bullets into the bodies of their fallen foes.

Chapter Twelve
RENO HILL

About four and a half miles upstream from Custer Hill, Reno's position occupied a shallow, saucerlike valley buttressed by a horseshoe ridge with the open end resting on the bluffs a hundred feet above the river. It faced the steep coulee up which he had led his troops and was exposed to rifle fire from ravines and nearby ridges, some of the latter higher than the place he had chosen to defend. Troop commanders, acting upon their own initiative, deployed their men around the perimeter with their animals and wounded in the center of the swale.

The troopers lay prone behind the meager shelter of their dismounted saddle packs, returning the sporadic fire of the Sioux sharpshooters who seemed, for the time being at least, willing to keep the fight alive without any concerted effort to attack in force. The soldiers speculated among themselves about the meaning of the haunting sound of distant gunfire. They had seen hundreds of warriors racing downstream but they had no way of knowing about the other hundreds already engaged in cutting the Custer command apart. Many of the junior officers were of the opinion that their chief was in real trouble and that something should be done about it at once. But Reno could not hear the muted battle clamor, and was equally deaf to their entreaties. He would make his move after, and only after, McDougall's pack train had caught up. At the moment he seemed more concerned with the dead than the living, for he sent a detachment of twelve men down to the river to recover and bury the body of Lieutenant Hodgson. They found Hodgson and Doctor De Wolf, but sniper fire was heavy enough to discourage the burial party. Back topside, Reno found the ammunition still had not arrived, so he sent Lieutenant Hare along the back trail to hurry it up. A detail under Varnum made a second attempt to reach Hodgson and encountered scout Herendeen, with a small group of survivors who had been left behind in the timber. The fact that they returned without the loss of a single man was in itself an ominous sign to at least some of the Reno command, that by far most of the hostiles were engaged elsewhere.

Meanwhile, Captain Weir, commander of D Company, which had been attached to Benteen, requested permission to lead his troop in an effort to locate Custer. When Reno's reply was negative, Weir decided to make a personal reconnaissance. Accompanied by his orderly, he rode out along the bluffs to the north for about a mile and a half beyond Reno Hill, to a point known now as Weir's Peak. Second Lieutenant Edgerly mounted D Company and followed his captain, a little to his right along the valley that paralleled the bluffs. From his vantage point, Weir could see Custer Ridge almost obliterated under a heavy pall of dust and smoke, with galloping, ghostly riders swirling about shooting into the ground. He also noted that large bands of them were turning away from the battlefield and swinging upstream, directly toward him. Seeing his own company trotting unwittingly toward certain destruction, he signaled Edgerly to join him on the bluffs.

Back on Reno Hill, Lieutenant Hare and four troopers from the pack train arrived, driving two ammunition-laden mules at a run. Hare was dispatched to Weir with orders for him to contact Custer, and that the entire command would follow as soon as the remainder of McDougall's train was brought up. Benteen, smarting under the delay, mounted companies H, K and M, and led them out on Weir's trail. Gradually, with or without orders from reluctant Reno, the remaining companies got under way. Their advance was hampered by the fact that many troopers by now had lost their horses. Too, the wounded had to be toted along on improvised blanket stretchers, for Indian fighters had learned of the horrible price paid by those left behind on the field of battle.

Today no one knows who, if any officer, gave the command to fall back. But the remnants of the "Seventh" had scarcely reached Weir's Peak when the decision was made to retire to their original defense position on Reno Hill. Unlike the recent headlong flight upstream, this withdrawal resembled a properly executed military maneuver. Companies M, D and K were dismounted and deployed at intervals along the route, to check the red assault, allowing the rest of the command to reach Reno Hill with few casualties. Here, at approximately seven o'clock in the evening of the twenty-fifth, the survivors of Custer's original command, numbering about 350 men (including civilian packers and many wounded troopers), faced three harrowing hours before sundown.

The three Crow scouts, Goes-Ahead, Hairy-Moccasin and White-Man-Runs-Him, reported in to Reno and then, sometime after sundown, slipped away to search out Terry. What they had heard and witnessed did nothing to raise the morale of a command fighting for its life. Although stubborn hearts of men and officers alike still refused to accept the obvious evidence that Custer was no more, anxious eyes strained northwestward now, looking for help from the Terry-Gibbon command. They got it from the cool conduct of one of their own, Captain Benteen, who later admitted that he had looked after things more than was his business or his duty.

From the Indian viewpoint, Sitting Bull's medicine was proving out. Twice, "Gray Fox" Crook had been whipped, three times Reno had been forced to retreat, "Long Hair's" day in the sun was ended, and "No Hips" Terry, struggling along the badlands that funneled the Big Horn River, was still too far away to worry about. The rocky ridges and ravines ringing Reno's horseshoe afforded plenty of cover for the rapidly growing hordes constantly crowding closer for the kill. There was standing room only for the late comers who witnessed a three-hour drama, from just beyond rifle range.

They saw their brothers, many of them using freshly-captured carbines, resting their guns on handy boulders or buffalo skulls, sighting carefully on exposed blueshirts, before squeezing the triggers. They watched others

sending arrows on curving trajectories into the middle of the swale where they could hardly fail to find targets. The Indians could have chosen any moment to overrun the command — but why risk it when it wasn't necessary? Soon enough, the soldier warriors would run out of water, and any who dared to take the 600-yard trail down through the heavily infiltrated coulee to the river would never return. Besides, they had counted many coups this day and there was much to boast about in the anticipated celebration down in the village. Tomorrow would be another day, when more blueshirts would tumble headfirst into their camp.

By the time the great red ball of the sun dropped below the western benchlands, Reno had to add eighteen killed and forty-six wounded to his casualty list.

Throughout the night of the 25th-26th, the beleaguered men on Reno Hill were constantly reminded by intermittent bursts of gunfire circling their perimeter that they had no place to go. Some troopers, wearied to exhaustion, drowsed in fitful catnaps in spite of the repeated song of victory, the quick beat of the tom-toms, and the high-pitched, keening notes of bereft women that accompanied the feasting and dancing in the great nomad city below. Most of them, using the few spades available, plus knives, tin cups, mess kits and even bare hands, dug rifle pits as best they could, anticipating full well the dismal challenge of daybreak.

Chapter Thirteen
HILL HOLE

AT THREE o'clock in the morning of the 26th, the black dome of the Montana sky paled in the east, bringing into third dimension the ghostly figures of men and horses on Reno Hill, and thousands of others climbing up from the prairie land. Dawn was the signal for renewed combat. And by the time true daylight flooded the landscape, it was already half obscured by the hot haze of battle. The Sioux and their Cheyenne allies were back in force to finish the job.

Dug in a little deeper now, the troopers behind their barricades of ration boxes and saddlepacks faced outward around the perimeter of their horseshoe position. From a hundred yards and beyond, in every direction, each rock and clump of sagebrush sheltered an exultant and determined warrior. However, as they had done the evening before, they seemed content to take a heavy toll without exposing themselves. Only a few reckless youngsters rode their ponies in wild, whooping forays, attempting to kill or count coup before swinging back into the ravines. As the white-hot sun rays

stabbed through the smoking hilltop into the parched throats of the soldiers, the need for water was more than they could bear — especially those who lay wounded in the open swale. Since no officer cared to order water carriers to certain death, a party of volunteers ran the coulee gauntlet down to the river and back. Some of them made it. One Indian account tells of a soldier, stripped to his underwear, who reached the stream and drank deeply at the bank where hostile bullets kicked up a spume that hid their target. Incredibly, he was able to rejoin the command.

135 • HILL HOLE

Then another miracle slowly unfolded. About noontime, the enemy fire slackened as many hundreds of Sioux and Cheyenne returned to their camp. Was it a trap to lure the soldiers from their hill-hole? There were still enough warriors on hand to stop a charge and send the troopers reeling back to their trenches. Could it be that Custer was once more distracting the enemy? Reno could not have had any such delusions, or he would have sent his scouts in search of his immediate commanding officer.

Whatever the reason for the gradual cessation of hostilities, as their shadows lengthened eastward, the survivors of the Seventh breathed easier, free for the moment at least, from the pressure of impending doom. They had no way of knowing that there was one great chieftain among those thousands of triumphant warriors who was thinking of the future. Enough white soldiers had tumbled upside down into his camp. A thousand of his horsemen were deployed in front of "No Hips" with his Gatling guns a few miles to the west. Even if those soldiers as well as the ones holed-out on the bluff were all killed, the long, vengeful arm from Washington would reach out relentlessly, bringing ever more bluecoats and more cannons. The wise Sitting Bull knew that in winning a great battle he might have lost a war. Perhaps if now, at the peak of victory, he called a stop to useless killing, he might conceivably make better terms for his people.

By late afternoon great clouds of black smoke billowed up from the bottom land as the Indians attempted to burn off the prairie grass. Shortly, the tepees were dismantled and bundled onto travois and a vast parade of men, women, children, dogs and ponies swarmed toward the distant Big Horn Mountains. The procession moved out in a close-knit formation, half a mile wide and three miles long. Reno's men, under the watchful eyes of hidden sharpshooters, gathered on the bluff and sent three cheers after the departing host.

139 · RENO HILL

At sunset, those horses and mules still able to walk were led down to the river, watered and allowed to graze. The men were given their first warm meal in two days, the wounded were tended, and the morale of the command rose to a new level. Early in the evening Scout Billy Jackson and Interpreter Girard struggled up from the bottom land, followed later by Private Thomas O'Neil and Lieutenant De Rudio. These men had spent over thirty harrowing hours after being cut off and left behind in the timber. Hidden in the deep thickets not far from the Uncpapa circle, they had heard the screams of dying men as the Indian women hunted down the wounded and dispatched them with knives and axes. Being downstream

from Reno Hill, they also heard the sounds of pitched battle floating down from Custer Ridge, followed by the off-key notes of a bugle in the hands of an untutored savage.

De Rudio told his fellow officers of a ghoulish incident. About daybreak on Monday morning had seen a gray-horse troop trotting along the bank of the Little Big Horn, led by a buckskin-clad figure wearing a big, white hat. Believing it to be a cavalry detachment under Tom Custer, De Rudio emerged from his place of concealment and shouted a greeting across the river. The reply was a hail of bullets that sent him scampering into the bushes. Luckily, the redskins mounted on gray cavalry horses and wearing newly acquired spoils of battle were on some urgent business and didn't tarry to hunt him down.

Chapter Fourteen
TERRY TURNS UP

ABOUT NINE O'CLOCK on the night of the 26th, Terry's column pitched camp in the form of a square in the valley of the Little Big Horn, eight miles downstream from Reno Hill. The heavy timber feathering the river which, at this point, swung across the wide valley from the eastern bluffs to the western benchlands, cut off the view upstream. But Lieutenant Bradley and his scouts up on the high ridges had watched the gathering of at least a thousand warriors preparing to contest any further advance. Earlier that day, the three inseparable Crow scouts — Goes-Ahead, Hairy-Moccasins and White-Man-Runs-Him — had found Bradley in the rough, ridge-bisected country between the Big Horn River and Tullock Creek. Their story of Custer's defeat had been dismissed as a report by frightened men who had witnessed only the beginning of the battle and had no understanding of Custer's ability to turn the tables. But the sense of foreboding inspired by the Crows increased as dispatches from their scouts kept filtering into Terry and Gibbon during the day. By now it was evident that there were plenty of Indians directly ahead of them, willing to face the fury of the dreaded Gatling guns. The great clouds of smoke spiraling up into the evening sky far beyond the crests of the cottonwoods *could* mean that Custer had followed through with his attack, had set the village afire and was now hot on the Indian trail. Then why the gathering of the red clans up ahead? A worried Terry didn't know the answer. Nor did Gibbon.

Early dawn of the 27th aroused Terry's restless command, only half recovered after the grueling night and day marches behind it. By the time the men had broken camp and were drawn up in battle formation, expectant and prepared for the worst, the scouts combing the flanks and the river timberland returned without having seen a single enemy. The valley floor, which looked deceptively flat, was cut by ravines and dry riverbeds. It was rough enough to slow a command encumbered with Gatling guns, tired pack mules and weary footsoldiers. But soon enough they saw the blackened prairie smoldering under a sooty haze upvalley where the great Indian camp had so recently stood.

Now only a couple of funeral lodges remained, surrounded by pony carcasses and the scattered debris of an abandoned encampment. Inside the tepees, the bodies of several warriors, painted and dressed in their finery, rested upon cottonwood scaffolds. The only signs of life were the snarling half-wolf dogs that resented the intrusion of the white man. The sightless eyes of three soldier's heads, scalped, burned and battered beyond recognition, looked down from the top of a lodgepole. Several headless and badly mutilated bodies were discovered as well as items of army clothing. A bullet-riddled buckskin shirt, identified as belonging to Lieutenant Porter, and a blood-soaked pair of drawers marked "Sturgis-Seventh cavalry" brought home the icy truth to all who saw them. It was confirmed as Lieutenant Bradley returned from a scout among the hills across the river.

"I have a very sad report to make," he said to Terry and Gibbon. "I have counted one hundred and ninety-seven bodies lying in the hills. I believe one of them to be that of General Custer."

Terry knew that roughly four hundred men of the original Custer column were missing. His immediate task was to account for them. Would he find them still alive and, if so, was he strong enough to rescue them? Would he find their naked bodies strewn over another lonely hilltop or burned to cinders on the valley floor — and be forced to turn his own fighting men into one enormous burial detail? The silence upstream was ominous. But with aching heart and with the certainty of victory dissipated by recent events, he ordered his troops once more into battle formation and proceeded up the west bank of the Little Big Horn.

A distant dust cloud rising from the ashes of the burned-out grasslands gave Reno's command the first indication of Terry's advance. Arikara scouts Forked-Horn and Young Hawk, followed by Lieutenants Hare and Wallace, were dispatched to establish contact and to lead the vanguard to Reno Hill. There, the news of Custer's defeat was received in shocked silence. Those who had suspected that their commander had met up with more than he could handle still couldn't visualize the complete annihilation of five companies or believe that the fabulous "Custer luck" had finally run its course.

There was much to be done. Terry set up camp on the west bank of the river, opposite the coulee leading up to Reno Hill. A field hospital was made ready to care for fifty-two wounded who were transported carefully in blanket litters. Detachments were sent out to look for and hopefully rescue any possible survivors of Custer's command. Other details were dispatched

to Custer Hill to identify the dead and to comb the river-bottom thickets for the missing men of Reno's command. Captain Benteen was ordered to follow Custer's trail in an effort to discover *how* the battle was fought and lost. Private Goodwin and Henry Bostwick galloped downstream to locate the *Far West* and order it to remain at the mouth of the Little Big Horn, ready to take aboard the wounded. Captain Ball with his company from the Second Cavalry Regiment followed the retreating Indian trail for fifteen miles until it split up, heading into the wild wilderness of the Big Horn mountains.

The detachments assigned to identify and later to bury the dead on Custer Hill had the most difficult job. The company roll lists were generally expected to be found in the pockets of the First Sergeants. But with one or two exceptions, the men were left stripped of any clothing. Many were scalped, their heads smashed in with axes, some with their feet cut off, others bristling with arrows, and still others marked by the Sioux with

slashes in the right thighs. Then, after the Indians had finished, nature in the form of a pitiless sun and swarms of voracious insects had taken over. After two days, the corpses were bloated and discolored beyond any hope of recognition. Identification of officers was a bit easier because their faces and figures were better known to the majority of troopers.

Custer carried a bullet wound in the left temple and another in the left breast, either of which could have been fatal. His body was found within a circle of dead horses near the highest point on Custer Ridge, surrounded by about forty of his men and most of his officers, Yates, Smith, Tom Custer, Reilly and Cooke. A bit farther down the south slope lay Keogh and Calhoun. Lieutenants Lord and Harrington were never identified and were

consequently listed as missing. Scout Mitch Bouyer's body was found near the river and by now his Crow wife, Magpie-Outside, had probably heard the news via "moccasin telegraph," and was chanting her song of sorrow.

By noon of the twenty-eighth, the burial details had finished their gruesome tasks. Thousands of items of Indian equipment were collected and burned. Litters were built to carry the fifty-two wounded and the expedition got under way, heading downstream this time. As they rode from the battlefield, Gibbon might well have recalled a parting jest to Custer, less than a week ago: "Don't be greedy. Save a few Indians for the rest of us." And Terry, remembering his message to Sheridan: "I hope one of the columns will find the Indians," was phrasing in his mind another one that was destined to stun the people of America.

Eight men were detailed to each of the fifty-two litters, which meant that over half of the Terry-Gibbon command, now totaling eight hundred men, were busy as bearers. The rough, uneven terrain made it difficult for the soldiers to carry their precious loads, and the progress became so slow that a halt was called to build horse-stretchers. Twenty-foot lodgepoles were fastened together by three-foot crosspieces, six feet apart. Horsehide lattice work and blankets covered the center sections and with a horse between the shafts at both ends, these workable ambulances needed only two attendants and were far more comfortable for the patients than the hand-toted variety.

On the move again, the space quickened for a while and then lagged as the moon disappeared at midnight and without lights of any kind and no indication of a trail to follow, pack mules, litters, Gatling guns, men and horses, stumbled blindly into one another. It was sunrise on the thirtieth when they met the *Far West* at the confluence of the two rivers. The wounded were immediately carried aboard, supplies unloaded for the rest of the command, and the boat steamed downstream, where it arrived at the Yellowstone base camp on the same day and fifty-three miles later. On July second, Terry and Gibbon concluded their overland expedition and ferried their troops across, to await reinforcements, additional supplies and further orders from General Sheridan.

Chapter Fifteen
HEADLINES

By now, unconfirmed rumors of the Custer debacle had spread far and wide across the land. Through the use of hand mirrors, smoke signals and relays of pony messengers, the Indians in their far-flung camps and agencies throughout the west, knew the truth. Although it was impossible for most

white men to accept a rumor that the great Custer might be dead, enough was believed to send a chilling wave of uncertainty flooding east of Missouri. Telegraph lines hummed with activity, determined editors demanded official word from Washington and, nationwide, anxious eyes looked toward Montana Territory.

On July 1, a civilian scout named "Muggins" Taylor, carrying dispatches from Terry and Gibbon, started west along a treacherous trail toward Fort Ellis. By the time he reached Horace Countryman's ranch on the Stillwater, he and his mount were both exhausted. So Countryman carried the word to Bozeman, where he found the government telegraph line down. He rode on to Helena, arriving in the middle of a Fourth of July celebration. Enough of the staff of the Helena *Daily Herald* were rounded up to produce an "extra," while the Western Union sparked the first white man's report eastward.

Fourteen wounded men who had recovered sufficiently to resume active duty were left behind at the Yellowstone base camp when the *Far West*, with thirty-eight patients aboard, raced downstream under full steam in a record-breaking 710-mile trip. At eleven o'clock in the evening of July fifth, she docked at Bismarck, Dakota Territory, with her derrick and jack staff draped in black and her flag at half-mast. Captain Marsh sped to the telegraph office and it was the nervous fingers of J. M. Carnahan that tapped out the message which officially confirmed the fact that the "Glorious Seventh" had been whipped within an inch of its life and that its famed commander, with every officer and man in five companies, had been killed.

Then the *Far West* made the short run to Fort Lincoln, where Captain Marsh left his precious cargo at the fort hospital and then turned to the tear-stained faces of many new widows and fatherless children. Among them was one who, with an intuitive premonition of disaster just fifty-one days before, had begged her husband to shear his long, yellow hair, for fear that it might tempt a scalper's knife. He had acquiesced.

Chapter Sixteen
AFTER THE BATTLE

FOLLOWING A great victory dance in the foothills of the Big Horn mountains, the tribes split up and went about the business of making a living — hunting buffalo. For a short time they were able to keep a jump ahead of the reinforced armies that had taken the field, bent upon removing the Indian menace for all time. Then retribution started catching up with the Indians when "Gray Fox" Crook surprised American Horse at Slim Buttes, Dakota Territory, and Colonel McKenzie caught Dull Knife's village wintering on Willow Creek.

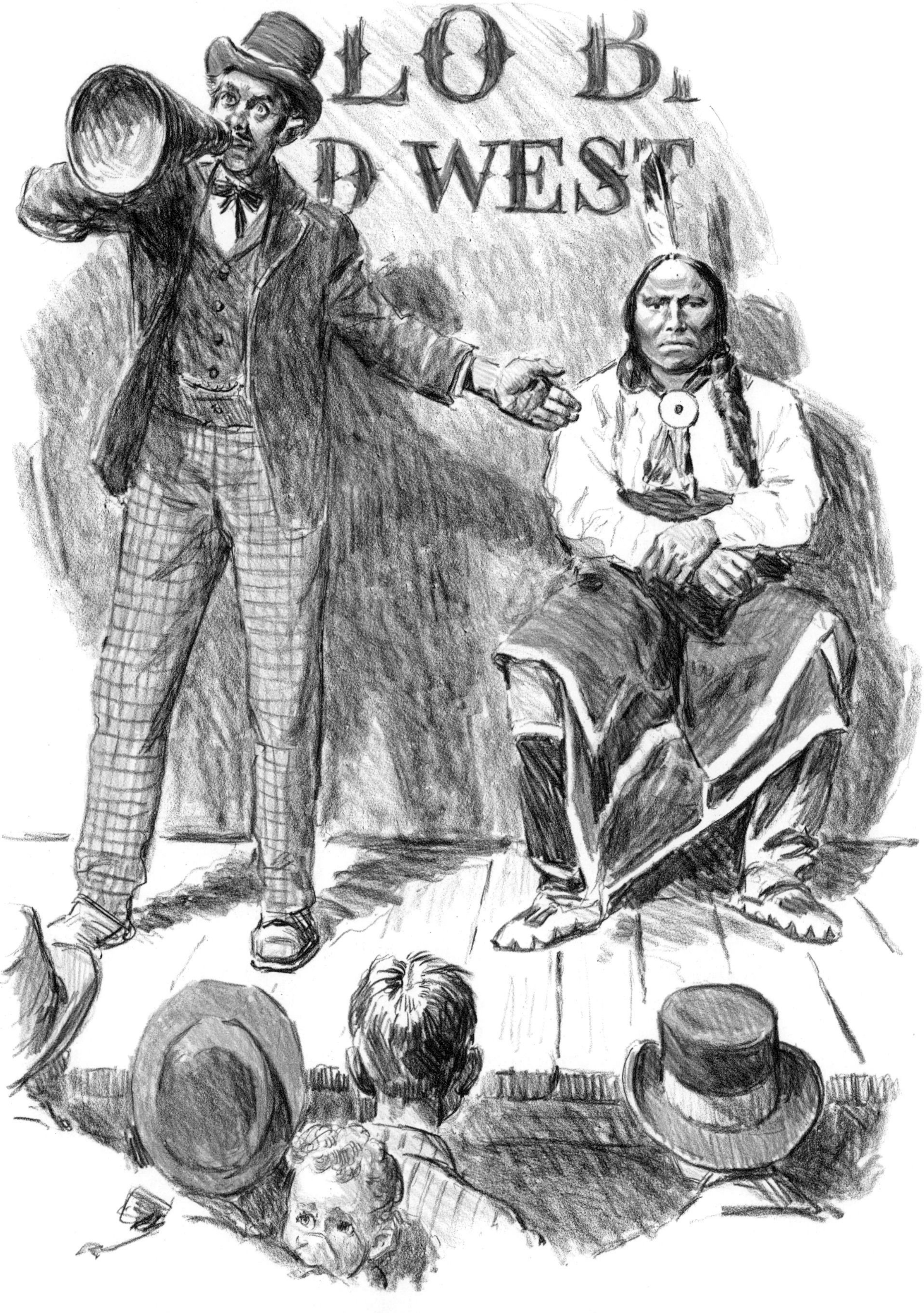
LO B
D WEST

As the bluecoat pressure increased, as he knew it would, Sitting Bull fled with his band into Canada. After four years, the constant threat of starvation among his people brought him back to Fort Buford, where he surrendered his diminished flock of 187 souls. The P. T. Barnum of the West, Colonel William (Buffalo Bill) Cody found him there and took him, along with Rain-in-the-Face and others, on a country-wide circus tour. However, show business offended the dignity of the aging warrior, and he soon returned to the Agency. There he heard of a new, strange cult, half-patterned after the white man's religion and half-pagan, called "The Ghost Dance." Its innovator, a Paiute medicine man named Wovoka who lived high in the Nevada hills, promised to bring back the buffalo and the old Indian way-of-life. It rekindled a spark of recalcitration in Sitting Bull and, for a while, he became one of the nominal leaders of the cult. The agent, James McLaughlin, fearing a general uprising, sent his Indian police to arrest the chief. During the resultant scuffle the greatest of all Indian leaders was shot to death.

Meanwhile the government people had been trying to persuade Crazy Horse to come into the Red Cloud reservation. Such a prison, even without walls, seemed the last place in the world for a man of his spirit. He would rather die. But his people were hungry, with most of the buffalo gone, and so, on the Moon-of-shedding-ponies (May), Crazy Horse led his unhappy followers to the agency. Later, his ailing wife, Black Shawl, asked him to take her to visit her own people at the Spotted Tail reservation. Believing that the chief was attempting to escape, fifty-five Indian scouts were sent to arrest him. He was taken to Fort Robinson where the master of decoy suddenly found himself trapped in a cell with barred windows. When he exploded into action, a soldier bayoneted him in the back — and another great American was gone.

Other Indians who had fought on Custer Ridge learned to walk the white man's road. It was a long, uphill twisting road for most of them. A freedom-loving warrior of the plains gained little recognition by growing the largest turnip on the agency farms. A new generation, born on the reservation, had to stifle the natural instinct for hunting and fighting. But Indians are not cast from the same mold, and some accepted their lazy fate while others learned to fight for peace, trying through the years to better the existence of their people. On each succeeding June 25th, at the Indian council on the battlefield, there were fewer warriors to relate their part in the struggle on Custer Ridge. In November 1955, Iron Hail (also known as Dewey Beard) died of natural causes. His was the last story echoing from the famous hilltop overlooking the Little Big Horn.

171 · AFTER THE BATTLE

Chapter Seventeen
ROUNDUP

Probably the nearest approach to the truth of what happened on Custer Ridge would have come from the pen of a trained reporter. But Mark Kellogg, "The-Man-Who-Makes-The-Paper-Talk," never had a chance to tell his story.

For a long time after the fight, the victors refused to talk for fear of reprisals by the government. But the Indian way of life demanded recognition for personal achievement in battle, and so gradually over the ensuing years great masses of evidence from the only eye-witnesses to the tragedy have been collected. Much of it is unreliable and contradictory for the Indians often were tricked into inaccuracy or exaggeration by the leading questions asked by probing reporters.

Unhappily, there were ignorance and prejudice among the men and officers who survived the campaign. First on the field, many of the immigrant soldiers were unable later to express in understandable English what they had found there. Their officers formed widely dissenting opinions as to *how* the battle was fought, how long it lasted, who was at fault, and so forth. Their conclusions were colored by the fact that they loved, respected, envied, or hated Custer, and also by a pride of regiment that cloaked family-feuding. Later, under oath, many of them reversed their original judgments.

Nevertheless, while the answers to many questions will never be solved to satisfy everybody, the preponderance of evidence from both red and white men points in a *probable* if not proven direction. For example: Who killed Custer? At least a dozen Sioux and Cheyennes at one time or another claimed or indicated that they had done so. Their statements had to be weighed against the known facts that many of Custer's officers were also clad in buckskins, some wore their hair long while his was shorn (on his last campaign), and there was a strong family resemblance among the Custer brothers. Any of the Indians could have made an honest mistake in identity amid the general confusion of battle.

A poetic version by Longfellow named Rain-in-the-Face as the killer, which notion was accepted and retracted by the chief himself several times during his lifetime. One Indian account tells of how Walking-Blanket-Woman's brother held Custer's arms while she stabbed him in the back. Obviously this had to be pure fiction *if* the white man's report that Custer's body was found with only two bullet wounds *and not otherwise mutilated* was indeed factual. The War Department's report could have been adjusted out of deference to Mrs. Custer's feelings. Otherwise, the long list of Custer slayers included Ice-Tan (Hawk), Flat-Hip, Two-Moon, Brave-Bear, Red-Horse, Brown-Back, Walks-Under-The-Ground, White-Bull, Harshay-Wolf, Big Nose and Medicine Bear.

To top it off, in 1909, at the last great Indian council at the Custer battlefield, wealthy Rodman Wannamaker offered a large cash award to be distributed among the Indians present, if they could name the actual, responsible party. The chiefs put their heads together and *elected* Brave-Bear of the Southern Cheyennes to carry the distinction. The probable answer was that even the Indians didn't know.

At what point did Custer meet his destiny? Long after the battle, Pretty-Shield, wife of Crow scout Goes Ahead (who saw at least the beginning of the fight), said she knew the answer. Her man told her that Custer, accompanied by "Mitch" Bouyer on one side and his personal standard-bearer on the other, was shot and killed in midstream, at Minneconjou Ford. If so, this might account for the statements of *some* military experts that the bodies of the command were scattered all over the field like corn, that the fight had turned into a leaderless buffalo hunt without any semblance of orderly withdrawal. But there was enough identification possible to mark the position of Smith's, Calhoun's and Keogh's skirmishers. This makes it probable that Custer was still alive and retaining control of his command until he reached the crest of the ridge where his body was found. After that, no one knows which of the forty-odd men and officers bunched together on that hilltop was last to perish.

The tales of survivors are legion, born of man's insatiable thirst for publicity. Some of them stemmed from troopers who were actually listed as members of the five companies, but who in fact were men on detached service at the base camp or with the pack train. The names of other claimants, many of them offering fantastic stories of escape, failed to tally with the official Army score card. Yet, with so many listed as "missing in action," it is still possible, after nearly a century, that an attic housecleaning somewhere in the land might produce a forgotten packet of letters or a memory book, with a credible story of survival. To date, except for the participating Indians, the only proven survivor to walk away from the battlefield was Captain Keogh's horse, Comanche. Although he was as severely wounded as many other mounts which were put out of their misery, Comanche recovered and lived comfortably to a ripe old horse age of twenty-four.

Why was the battle lost? Was it Custer's fault? If he had followed his orders to the letter and scouted the upper Rosebud before following the Indian trail over the Wolfe divide, would Terry and Gibbon have arrived on the far side in time to catch the entire camp between them? Highly improbable — because of the lack of today's means of instant communication. Inter-command couriers, delayed for hours or even days because of the rough nature of a practically unknown region infested with hostiles, could hardly be relied upon to help pull off a joint attack by such widely separated forces.

Was Custer to blame for splitting his own command and thereby getting himself into a spot where he couldn't use all of his striking power effectively? In doing so, he violated an accepted principle of warfare. But Indian fighting inspired new rules and, as a renowned Indian fighter, he made them. He had split his command before, successfully, and had confidence that it would work again.

Was Reno responsible when he failed to follow through with his original attack? Or when he charged the wrong way and released Gall's hordes to work-over Custer? Conceivably he might have changed the outcome of the battle — or he too could have been wiped out. Monday-morning quarterbacks who labeled Reno coward *knew* he was facing only a rear-guard action but at the time, Reno had cause to believe that he was up against more than he could handle.

How about Benteen, when he stopped to rescue Reno and so failed to rejoin Custer, as ordered? Up on the bluffs, he acquitted himself as an abler officer than Reno, but by the time he took the bit in his teeth, Custer didn't need him. Benteen, too, was stopped dead in his tracks and forced to retire.

These questions and countless more which arose immediately after the battle have been subject to controversy and speculation down through the years. They have been bandied about by the press, debated by military experts, romanticized by poets, become the subject matter of enough books to stock a library, furnished tests for classroom cadets, and have caused ceaseless arguments by the defenders and detractors of the men involved. They can never be answered to the complete satisfaction of everyone concerned.

In books and articles, Mrs. Custer carried the torch for her husband. And as Custer's flame burned brighter even after death, Reno suffered as the scapegoat. When he demanded a court martial, he was acquitted on all counts, but the smear wouldn't rub off — even with alcohol.

A century later, the only sure if admittedly oversimplified reason for Custer's defeat was that no one, from Sheridan, Terry, Custer, on down to the lowliest private, realized the determination of Sioux and Cheyenne to stand and fight. The only wonder of it was that the Indians failed to finish off Reno's troops and the Terry-Gibbon command while they had the chance. In all probability, they had the power and the emboldened spirit to do just that.

SELECTED BIBLIOGRAPHY

Brininstool, E. A. *A Trooper with Custer*. Columbus, O., 1926.

Custer, Elizabeth B. *Boots and Saddles*. New York, 1885.

Custer, George A. *My Life on the Plains*. Chicago, 1952.

Dustin, Fred. *The Custer Tragedy*. Ann Arbor, 1939.

Fougera, Katherine G. *With Custer's Cavalry*. Caldwell, Ida., 1940.

Graham, Col. William A. *The Custer Myth*. Harrisburg, 1953.

Hunt, Frazier and Robert. *I Fought with Custer*. New York, 1947.

Marquis, Thomas B. *A Warrior Who Fought Custer*. Minneapolis, 1931.

Parsons, John E. and Dumont, John S. *Firearms Used in the Custer Battle*. Harrisburg, 1953.

Sandoz, Mari. *The Battle of the Little Bighorn*. New York, 1966.

——. *Crazy Horse*. New York, 1955.

Stewart, Edgar I. *Custer's Luck*. Norman, Okla., 1955.

Van de Water, Frederick F. *Glory Hunter*. Indianapolis, 1934.

Vestal, Stanley. *Sitting Bull*. Boston, 1932.

INDEX

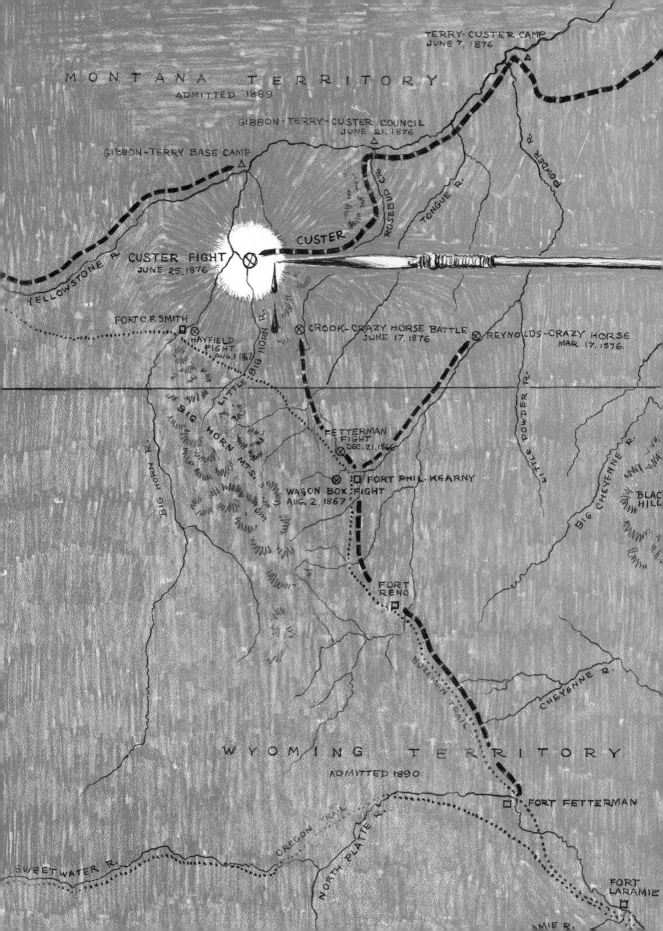

MONTANA TERRITORY
ADMITTED 1889

TERRY-CUSTER CAMP
JUNE 7, 1876

GIBBON-TERRY-CUSTER COUNCIL
JUNE 21, 1876

GIBBON-TERRY BASE CAMP

POWDER R.

ROSEBUD CR.

TONGUE R.

CUSTER

CUSTER FIGHT
JUNE 25, 1876

YELLOWSTONE R.

LITTLE BIG HORN R.

FORT C.F. SMITH

HAYFIELD
FIGHT
AUG. 1, 1867

CROOK-CRAZY HORSE BATTLE
JUNE 17, 1876

REYNOLDS-CRAZY HORSE
MAR. 17, 1876

LITTLE POWDER R.

BIG HORN R.

BIG HORN MTS.

FETTERMAN
FIGHT
DEC. 21, 1866

FORT PHIL KEARNY

WAGON BOX FIGHT
AUG. 2, 1867

BIG CHEYENNE R.

BLACK HILL

FORT
RENO

BOZEMAN TRAIL

CHEYENNE R.

WYOMING TERRITORY
ADMITTED 1890

FORT FETTERMAN

OREGON TRAIL

SWEETWATER R.

NORTH PLATTE R.

FORT
LARAMIE

AMIE R.